BANDANNA
BOOK

BY TY JUAN AHN

CIDER MILL
PRESS

BOOK
PUBLISHERS

KENNEBUNKPORT, MAINE

13 Digit ISBN: 978-1-933662-81-7
10 Digit ISBN: 1-933662-81-6

This book may be ordered by mail from the publisher. Please include $2.75 for postage and handling. Please support your local bookseller first!

Books published by Cider Mill Press Book Publishers are available at special discounts for bulk purchases in the United States by corporations, institutions, and other organizations. For more information, please contact the publisher.

Cider Mill Press Book Publishers
"Where good books are ready for press"
12 Port Farm Road
Kennebunkport, Maine 04046

Visit us on the web!
www.cidermillpress.com

Concept Creator: Toby Schmidt
Design by Jessica Disbrow
Printed in China

1 2 3 4 5 6 7 8 9 0
First Edition

TABLE OF CONTENTS

PERHAPS THE IDEA OF AN ACTUAL BOOK ON BANDANNAS AND ITS MANY USES SEEMS RIDICULOUS TO YOU.

Maybe you think the tree pulp used for this project could have been put to better use toilet papering the White House. If you think that–congratulations! You are just the person for which this book is intended. A free thinker, a person with bold opinions, someone who doesn't mind expressing the inner rebel and laughing in the face of tradition. While the cover may belie its intent, this book is not just about bandannas. It is really about you. You now own something that holds the key to your self-expression. Talk about cult followings–the bandanna has not one, but many. Wearing one, regardless where or how, says so much, but

★ ★

most importantly, it says 'individuality.' Even if you are in a stadium full of bandanna-wearing bikers, you will stand out as unique and apart from the pack precisely because you are wearing a bandanna. Perhaps because of that very reason, it has become a staple to the expression of the ideal of self identity. No one wants to be a conformist, even those who know no other way because they've spent their lives sucking up to authority. In the heart of every person is the seed of an individualist. And this simple thing—really, this small square of fabric—has the ability to water that seed.

Wrapping it around your head to cover your bald spot or shoving it in the breast pocket of your silk suit tells the world that you dare to be different. In and of itself, as a fashion statement, there is no other as versatile and widely accepted piece of gender-neutral clothing that has been worn by so many and says so much about the wearer. And it's also a darned handy thing to own, which you will find out later. It's been said that the monogrammed hanky is for show and the bandanna is for blow, but this book roundly debunks that. Not only is the form and function of the bandanna perfect, it's also cool—as in trendy, hip, vogue, dapper, stylin', hot, mod, now, the bomb, even groovy for you hippies. And it will remain forever that way because it is a staple of any wardrobe—as timeless as time itself, as fashionably fundamental as white socks and as American as rock n' roll and obesity. While it is much imitated, it has

★ ★

never truly been replaced, and many have tried—the kerchief, hanky, snot rag, do rag, scarf, and even burqa have not quite reached the level of popularity as the bandanna.

So, Congratulations. You are now the owner of the only piece of fabric that you will ever need. Still not convinced? Skeptical, are you? Well, read on MacBeth. And after you're done turning the last page, if you are not convinced that the 22" by 22" paisley swatch of cloth you hold in your hand isn't the most useful, adaptable, ultra-multi-functional item you have ever seen, well...that would be a shame.

DID YOU KNOW?

There is a National Bandanna Day in Australia! That's right. CanTeen, the Australian Organisation for Young People Living with Cancer, is the national support organisation for young people based in Australia. It has adopted the bandanna as its national symbol because so many cancer patients use a bandanna to cover their heads during chemo because of hair loss.

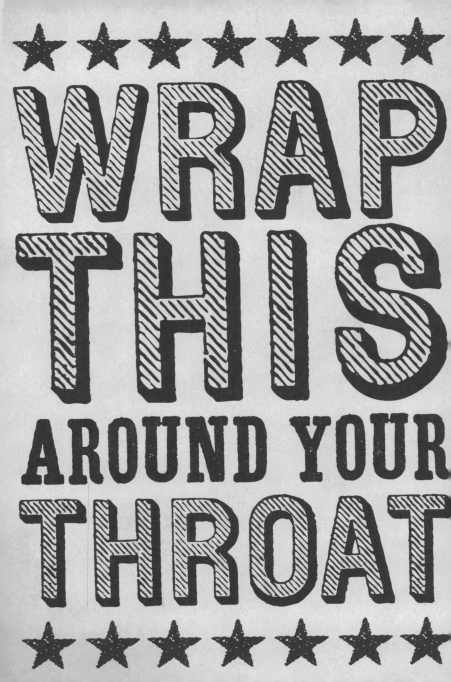

CHAPTER 2

From nooses to neckties,

men and the women who love or hate them – or both -- have been tying things around their necks since the beginning of time. Given how long ago the beginning of time was and all the fashion trends that have come and gone, the bandanna is relatively new to the fashion scene. And if anthropologists are correct about when primitive man first appeared on this planet, that means leafing through about seven million years of back issues of *Vogue* magazine. Thankfully for us, early primitive man limited his accessorizing to crudely carved clubs, and there was little concern over neckwear. But there are those socio-historians who contend that neckwear can find its roots buried in the tribal doings of our hairy ancestors. Of course, this isn't proven, but some suggest that prehistoric humans, not unlike apes, had to puff up and pound their chests to gain some respect, and exert their authority. It could be that the rank of the top male often depended on how well he was able to exhibit his prowess with this infernal chest beating.

Based on this, one could then logically make the assumption that the need to have something adorn the neck, which brings attention to the chest--the center of power--is directly tied to man's primal lust for control and the need to dominate. While much of this is conjecture, there could be some credibility to the theory, because one glance into the archives of popular American television finds some pretty compelling evidence. After all, Fred Flintstone wore a tie.

★ ★ ★

DID YOU KNOW?

Some speculate that bandito comes from the word bandanna, since bandits often wore them as masks to conceal their identities.

✳ OLÉ ✳

★ ★

THE BIRTH OF NECKWEAR

ALL OF THAT HEADY TALK ASIDE,
the earliest form of recorded neckwear appears in ancient
Rome. History tells us that it was the fashion of Roman
public speakers—read, statesmen— to wear neck cloths to
protect their throats, keeping them warm so that they could
pontificate for hours, albeit days, on end. Thankfully,
today's politicians have abandoned that fashion trend,
therefore exposing their throats to the cold and elements,
and hopefully rendering them speechless (or strangled) by
today's neckties. Roman soldiers also adopted neck cloths,
as did soldiers from ancient China, to add some much-
needed padding before they put on their armor. In all these
cases, neck clothes were worn not for show but for function.
The need for functionality drove the minimal neckwear use
in the Middle Ages. It might have been the superstition
that bodily ills entered one through the throat that had
something to do with the continued popularity of a protective
neckcloth, or perhaps soldiers felt more secure having their

★ ★ ★ ★ ★ ★ ★ ★ ★ ★ ★ ★ ★ ★ ★ ★ ★ ★ ★ ★

neck covered in battle. Or maybe they were just cold.

It wasn't until the mid-1600s that the fashion scene embraced the idea of neckwear as a must-have accessory for men. Thanks to the reign of the infamous dandy, Louis XIV of France -- who also ushered in the mad male craze of wearing colorful tights, voluminous lace collars and flamboyant tower wigs. Legend has it that a regiment of crack Croatian mercenaries, who were celebrating their victory over the Turks, visited France and were presented as heroes to King Louis. The vain king, known for his compulsion for fashion, noticed that the officers wore brightly colored silk handkerchiefs around their necks. The king was so enthralled with these that he made them a royal insignia and created his own regiment of Royal Cravattes. (The French word cravat comes from the Croatian, "kravate.")

Given the seal of approval by the French fashion maven and harbinger of haute couture, the new fashion quickly spread to other countries. It is said that when Napoleon wore white silk handkerchiefs around his neck in battle, he always won. At Waterloo, he wore a white cravat, not a hanky, and lost the battle and his kingdom. Oh well.

Thanks to high-profile men like him, regardless of their overall success rates in battle, cravats become standard issue. English gentlemen always wore some type of cloth around their necks, and the more elegant the better. Cravats were fashioned from plaid, embroidered linen, and other fabrics.

They were often decorated with ribbon bows, lace, and tasseled string. Some were so high that a man couldn't turn his head, while others were thick enough to stop a sword thrust, which came in pretty handy during a duel.

★ ★ ★

ENTER BEAU BRUMMEL

PERHAPS NO FASHIONISTA is more closely tied to neckwear than the Englishman Beau Brummel, the veritable father of modern neckties and maybe very distant, second grand uncle-once-removed to the bandanna. Born George Bryan Brummell and not of royal or privileged birth, Brummell was able, through hearty pandering, to rise in the ranks of England's elite and make his mark on, of all places, their wardrobe. He focused on the cravat – developing complex and elaborate knots for varying social events and times of day, and catapulting this bit of fabric to a fashion statement in and of itself. By the late 1800s, there were over 32 ways to fashionably knot a cravat. Considered the father of dandyism, he claimed to take five hours to dress, and recommended that his boots be polished with champagne. The effectiveness of this as a shoe polish has yet to be proved. But like most superficial dandies, he was his own undoing. He incurred a lot of gambling debt and managed to insult the wrong person. (He supposedly said to a peer, "Who's your fat friend?" That friend was the Prince of Wales.) He fled to France where, years later, he died penniless of insanity thanks to a bad bout of syphilis. Guess the cravat and champagne might not have helped.

★ ★ ★

DID YOU KNOW?

The red bandanna is the most popular color of traditional bandanna sold.

ACROSS THE SEA

AS ALL SUPER MODELS KNOW, when fashion is this important, it cannot be stopped. The cravat, even with Brummel's sad end, spread across the modern world of the 17th century, and across the Atlantic Ocean to the colonists in America, who, like their love of tea, eventually rebelled against all things English and chose to abandon the cravat for the simple bow tie and, eventually, the necktie. In search of their own independence but never having the guts to actually create something of their own, they stumbled upon a fashion that they could steal—the bandanna.

In truth, the bandanna was not born from the inbreeding of the cravat and a woman's hanky. No, it actually came from India. Well, at least the word and the fabric from which the original bandannas were made did. There are two schools of thought as to the origins of the word "bandanna." One is that it is derived from the Sanskrit word, bandhna, or bandhana, meaning "tying." The other is that it was borrowed either from Hindustani (which was the lingua franca of traders before India's independence) or from Bengali, the language of the region in which bandannas were made. In both languages the word means tie-dyed-- the technique by which small sections of cloth are tightly wrapped with thread to prevent the dye from penetrating those parts, and thereby creating distinct patterns.

DID YOU KNOW?

As most know, the bandanna has morphed into significant fashion wear for gangs, most of whom consider it the flag of their gang nation. Color depicts which gang you belong to, and if you happen to wander into gang territory innocently wearing a bandanna and don't happen to be a member of any gang, much less the gang you ran into, you are in a heap of trouble. Not very comforting for those of us with babushka-wearing Bosnian grandmothers living in East L.A.

★ ★

NECKWEAR OR HANKY?

WE HAVE THE DUTCH EAST INDIA COMPANY,

established in 1602, to thank for the booming bandanna industry. From its trading station north of Calcutta, the Dutch East India Company's initial trade in bandannas was to Europe in the early eighteenth century. The Dutch called these textiles "taffa de foolas" (taffeta silk neckcloths – no, not scarves for fools), but they were put to many uses and found a ready market in Europe.

Like any good fashion product, these handkerchiefs were soon copied by European textile weavers and dyers and sold by merchants who pressured their country's governments into protecting their imitations from competition by the imported originals. These are called "knockoffs" today. Funny how the more things change the more they stay the same.

By 1720, the British East India Company also began exporting bandannas from its trading station in Calcutta.

★ ★ ★ ★ ★ ★ ★ ★ ★ ★ ★ ★ ★ ★ ★ ★ ★ ★ ★

Since by this time it was already illegal to sell the Indian-made bandannas in England, the BEIC re-exported them from England to the American colonies. The new Americans gobbled them up like maize. With multiple uses from hankies to wash cloths, and oh so affordable, the demand grew.

By the late eighteenth century, tens of thousands of bandannas were imported from India to New England on American ships. It is estimated that over the course of that century, over seven million bandannas were manufactured, first overseas in India and then later in America.

DID YOU KNOW?

Bandannas were a fashion must for the four most famous cartoon turtles of the 1980s. Can you name the color of the bandannas that each of the Teenage Mutant Ninja Turtles wore? Better yet, can you even name them?

Leonardo - blue

Raphael - red

Michaelangelo - orange

Donatello - purple

FUN TO WEAR – AND SO MANY USES

THE BANDANNA WAS EASILY ADAPTABLE,

something Americans loved and therefore developed all sorts of uses for. In the early days, these simple squares were used as handkerchiefs and neckerchiefs, head wraps, and bundle wraps. They were made of many fabrics in many patterns and colors and were imported not only from India but from China, England, and Europe. Men loved them as hankies. Thanks to the popularity of snuff—finely ground tobacco inhaled through the nose, which also created a dark, unpleasant discharge—there was an increased need for handkerchiefs, particularly the dark-colored ones. It wasn't long before bandannas started cropping up everywhere in America. Sailors customarily wore a neckerchief, which was often a bandanna. African American women, known as slaves at the time, usually wore bandannas, which were also known as kerchiefs, head-kerchiefs, hand handkerchiefs, and turbans. Before the American industrial revolution began in the textile mills of New England, Indian cotton goods were in great demand for everyday uses. Indian silk bandannas were imported and priced for most townsfolk, competing with British imports and home manufactures. When the Industrial Revolution hit, the bandanna became a wholly domesticated product, and trade with India dropped off. Now they're all made in China.

⭐ ⭐ ⭐

DID YOU KNOW?

Bandanna is also a language. It has morphed into a type of code, known as hanky code, which is used primarily in the gay community to indicate particular sexual references. Where the bandanna is worn, either in the right or left pocket, and its color can be translated to have varying meaning. The problem is, not everyone understands the code, which can cause a lot of confusion.

RIDE 'EM COWBOY

THE BANDANNA MIGRATED ONTO THE WIDE OPEN SPACES OF THE WILD, WILD WEST,

where it became practically indispensable, and where its place as part of American history was permanently sealed. Initially, the bandanna was pulled up over the mouth to keep dust off the face and out of the mouths of the rough and ready. From there it took on a life of its own with the pioneers and their new lifestyle, becoming part of the true fabric of the land and morphing into many uses where the deer and antelope played. Banditos picked up on this fashion trend, realizing that if half the face— the recognizable half—is covered, the bandanna could be used as a mask, ultimately padding their own wallets. Red or blue bandannas were the original colors of choice.

★ ★

Today, bandannas have become the staple of any self-respecting school boy dressing up as a cowpoke for Halloween. But what young and old man alike doesn't dream of riding the range and living the western lifestyle? And while many youngsters only get to dress up as cowboys, for plenty of folks the cowboy tradition—and attire that includes a bandanna – is a way of life. For them, the bandanna still keeps out the dust and dirt while not only looking good, but providing a simple yet essential piece of fabric for doing all kinds of things like the ones in this book (and many more yet to be invented).

The bandanna uses honed by taming the wild, wild west have been adapted and, quite frankly, stolen by the growing number of outdoorsmen and naturalists. No self-respecting Boy Scout would enter the woods without pocketknife, canteen and bandanna. From tourniquet to toilet paper, the bandanna has so many emergency uses in the natural world, it's a wonder that civilization got this far without it.

DID YOU KNOW?

Possibly one the most famous and recognizable cowboys of the 20th century media -Hopalong Cassidy- made the long red bandanna synonymous with cowboy lore, thanks to his popular series of movies and radio talk show. According to the book series written by Clarence Mulford in the 1930s, Hoppy lived on the Bar 20 ranch in Northwestern Texas, near the town of Buckskin- population 100. And in every movie he made, with or without sidekick, he always wore his red bandanna, cutting quite a figure on the wide open range.

100 USES

From the obvious to the sublime, the bandanna has seen and done it all.

CHAPTER 3

SLAVE TO FASHION

ACCESSORIES AND DOO DADS FOR YOUR DO RAG. FROM HEAD GEAR TO NECK WEAR

1.

TRADITIONALIST

Wear the bandanna for its original intent—as a sassy neck accessory. Tie it around your neck, wear the knot in back for that early cowpoke look. Slide the knot in front if you're aching to look like a gondolier. Or slip it off to the side if you can't make up your mind.

★ ★ ★

★ ★

2.

HIPPIE DOG

What dog hasn't been born to run? Shake loose the boring old dog collar with tags and let pup be the free spirit he was intended to be. Simply knot the bandanna at the very ends after measuring for fit, and slip it around his hairy neck. Put him on the back of your hog and go see **America**.

★ ★

3.

⊛ THE ⊛
I LOVE MY PONYTAIL
HAIR TIE

Knot it around your thick shock of blonde hair, nice and high on the back of your head, for that country-girl-at-the-fair look. Make it nice and tight to remove any excess facial wrinkles, and show the world that the fifties are indeed very much alive.

★ ★

4.

the FAUX APACHE

If tie dye is still a big part of your wardrobe and peace signs never grew old, then this look is for you. Fold the bandanna in one-inch increments, and tie it around your forehead, knot in back, over your hair. Try not to wash your hair for several days to capture the true Willie Nelson in you.

5.

WATCH THIS 👉

Nothing says 'hang loose, man' for your Type A personality quite like replacing the alligator watchband on your Rolex with a bandanna. Just slide the fabric through the end pins, and wrap the rest of the cloth around your wrist.

(Note: This is perfect for vacations in warmer climates. But if you really want to pretend you are relaxing, just wrap the bandanna over your watch, so no one is the wiser. That way you can still look laid back, while you secretly obsess over time.)

★ ★

6.

DRESS IT UP

Carefully folded, the bandanna can do as much if not more than the hanky when it comes to men's fashion. Nothing says sophisticate like a pocket square. Whether it be the presidential fold—folding the bandanna at right angles to fit in the pocket-or the **TV** fold—which looks similar but is folded diagonally with the point inside the pocket—the bandanna adds that bit of avant garde to any suit and occasion.

★ ★

7.

DRESS IT
DOWN

If you prefer Levi's to Armani, try the
above folds, but stuff the bandanna in
your back pocket, for the well-groomed,
yet casual male look.

★ ★ ★

8.

BABY
maybe?

If Junior wets through his diaper and there is no store in sight, rest assured. Having a spare bandanna can save the day. Just fold the fabric diagonally, slide it under baby's bottom, and bring the middle piece through baby's legs, knotting the remaining two ends in front and around the third piece. Happy, dry and stylin'.

9. & 10.

drool catcher

Introduce Junior to the joys of cowboy hood and keep his chest dry by folding the bandanna in two diagonally, and tying it around his neck. Perfect for keeping his shirt free of mashed turnip.

baby wiper

If you're a smart parent who plans ahead, you'll have several bandannas with you, just in case baby makes a big mess and needs some clean up before donning his new paisley diaper.

★ ★

11.

BOOTIES

TO YOU ✳

Booties never looked so good as they do when they're made of bandannas. These fabric bits can act as custom-made shoes, perfect to keep toes warm during long trips lassoed into a car seat by free-wheeling parents criss-crossing the country in the VW bus.

✪ ✪ ✪

★ ★

12.

IN-A-PINCH
UNDERWEAR

✪ ✪ ✪

O O O P S

Forgot to do the laundry?

Try tying a bandanna around your hips,
á la the baby diaper, and feel confident
all day long.

✪ ✪ ✪

★ ★

13.

JEAN PATCH

Nothing says down-home more than using your bandanna to fix those unsightly thin spots on the butt or knees of your worn-out jeans. If you use them copiously, you will have a pair that is all bandanna, kept together by bits and pieces of jean.

14.

AHOY
MATEY

Pirate never goes out of style. Bring back privateering in a big way by wearing your bandanna knotted to one side over your ear, which of course should be adorned with a big gold hoop earring and an annoying parrot.

★ ★ ★

15.

DO
RAG

Or you could come back to this century by flipping the knot to the back of your skull, creating your own do-rag. Slap on your baseball cap, **WWI** helmet with the silver spike, or rock climbing helmet, and you are ready for just about anything.

16.

HALTER TOP

Combine the home-spun look with the fashion must-have backless halter top. If you are narrow of back, just take the fabric and fold it in half, diagonally, and tie the two ends around your back. If you aren't, use two or three.

★ ★

17.

Babushka

If it was good enough for your immigrant great grandmother, it's good enough for you. The babushka is different from the American kerchief in that it is tied under one's chin, while the kerchief is tied under one's hair at the back of the neck, keeping ears exposed to the wind. Not very helpful in Siberia.

✪ ✪ ✪

★ ★ ★ ★ ★ ★ ★ ★ ★ ★ ★ ★ ★ ★ ★ ★ ★ ★ ★ ★

18.

Get thee 👉 TO A NUNNERY

In a pinch, the bandana also doubles as a handy veil, for those devout in faith, who want to keep the crowns of their heads covered out of respect. Just toss it on your head as is and start praying.

★ ★ ★

★ ★ ★ ★ ★ ★ ★ ★ ★ ★ ★ ★ ★ ★ ★ ★ ★ ★ ★ ★

19. & 20.

GANG WEAR

If you fancy you're a member of the Crips, you might want to don a blue bandanna under your sideways-fitting baseball cap, barely touching the bling around your neck.

THIGH HIGH

There was a time when wearing a bandanna on your thigh spelled 'c-o-o-l.' Reliving the Chachi "Happy Days" era might be fun, if not offbeat. Or was that Punky Brewster? Just pick a thigh, any thigh, and tie one on.

21.

BANDANNA
TOTE BAG

Be the first on your block to own one!

How to do it:

You need three bandannas for this, and no sewing machine. Lay two bandanas out, wrong sides together; cut a slit every 3/4" cutting up to the most inner printed square on the bandana (Figure 1). Cut out the corners. Flip them over, right sides facing out (Figure 2). Beginning at one of the corners, take one of the fringes from the top and one from the bottom and tie them together in a double knot. Tie one on each corner. Continue tying all around except for the top (Figure 3). This will be left open. To make the handle, cut one bandanna into eight strips. Discard all but three. braid them, knotting at each end (Figure 4). Knot an end to each side of the bag (Figure 5). Iron the top fringes down on each side.

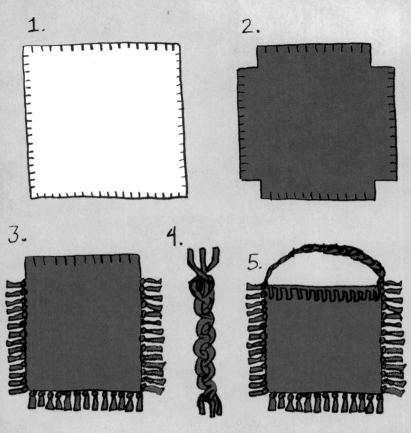

VOILA !

* *

22.

HOBO
HANDBAG

Lest we forget, the bandanna was the original suitcase for bums bumming a ride on the rails, once called a bindle-stick for those word purists. Revive this traditional way of travel by selecting a slim and refined old branch, about three feet long. Stuff all your worldly belongings into a laid out bandanna, and then tie the edges securely at the far end. Toss it over your shoulder, smear some coal dust on your face, and get on the busy end of your thumb.

23.

Shoulder
PADS

OK, it's not the 80s but who says you have to be a conformist to fashion. It could be. At least, on your shoulders. Get that Norma Kamali height to your frame by folding two bandannas into small squares, and inserting them under your favorite blouse or sweater. Might give you the heft you need.

24. & 25.

CHEST ENHANCER

Tired of your front looking like your back? When scrunched up, the bandanna can add two cup sizes to your frame. A perfect C cup.

GARTER BELT

Always carry a blue one in case of a shotgun wedding. Fills the bill for old, new, borrowed and blue.

★ ★

26.

WHO SAID
rag curls are out?

Not Shirley Temple, that's for sure. Rip the bandanna into one-inch strips, and tie up your wet hair in knots right before sleeping. Take some aspirin, too, to help with that headache you'll have in the morning from sleeping on bandanna knots all night long.

★ ★ ★

27.

HAT BAND

Add some zest to your straw hat. Anyone can add cockatiel feathers and fruit to their head apparel, but it takes a real maverick to tie a bandanna around the crown of your hat. Dare to be different.

28.

BROOCH
pin holder

You can never have too many brooches.
Well, at least your grandmother couldn't.
The vexing problem is how to transport
them. Pin them to a bandanna and guess
what? Problem solved.

★ ★ ★

* * * * * * * * * * * * * * * * * * *

29.
TIE-DYE
IS BACK

And some will contend it never was out. Fresh, new bandannas contain enough dye to leach into just about any garment. Take out your rubber bands, and tie them around whatever white garment you would like tie-dyed, and throw it all in the hot water, soak cycle. In a matter of 20 minutes, you will be amazed at what you have done.

30. & 31.

BLINDFOLD

Tired of everyone knowing how to get to your house? Next time you pick up a pal to come over for a game of Mahjong and spiced tea, tie a blindfold around her eyes. You'll protect your privacy and she has a thrill of a lifetime. Or just use it over your eyes for a restful sleep.

EMERGENCY
FEMININE NAPKIN

In a pinch, you'll find nothing better. Trust us. We're professionals.

32.
NECK
COVER

How do you protect your neck from the damaging rays of the sun? Ouch. You open your bandanna, place it on your head, with most of the cloth hanging over the back of your neck, and stick a ball cap on. Works like a charm. And folks might think you're a sheik.

33.

Monty Python
HAT WEAR

Knot the corners tight enough so the cap fits snugly on your head. It's a look, but not one that will win you too many friends. Don't forget to say,

"My brain hurts."

⭐ ⭐ ⭐

34.

TO BELT OR NOT TO BELT

Depending on your girth, more than one bandanna might do the trick. Just tie the ends in knots and slide it through your loops. Or wear it like a sassy sash on your hips, or the side of your head if you're from East **LA**.

EAR
MUFFS

Wrapped just right around the outside of the hair, the bandanna is just the right size and thickness to act as a pretty darned good set of ear muffs. Not to mention, they're fetching as well.

★ ★

36.

EYE
PATCH

Either for fashion or medical reasons,
bandannas have been successfully used
as eye patches, as well as mouth and face
protectors in sandstorms – a real problem in
most countries. Keep your friends guessing.
Wear one to dinner tomorrow night.

★ ★ ★

★ ★

A MUST FOR YOUR RIDE

VEHICULAR USES

No doubt about it. A bandanna is a must-have for your glove compartment. Simply put: Don't leave home without it.

Antenna ALERT

Tying a bandanna on your car's antenna, providing you have a car that has one, says you are hippy friendly. Or, if it breaks down, it indicates that you are in distress. Or make it a snap to find your car in a crowded lot. No antenna? Try your side view mirror, your tailpipe or your fender.

★ ★ ★ ★ ★ ★ ★ ★ ★ ★ ★ ★ ★ ★ ★ ★ ★ ★ ★

38.

STEER CLEAR

A red bandanna makes the perfect warning for drivers behind you when you are carrying long, wooden 2' by 4's. Tie it on the end to make sure you don't decapitate the guy behind you with a sudden stop.

★ ★ ★

★ ★

39. & 40.

LOST
GAS CAP

Use your bandanna to plug the hole. And good luck getting a new gas cap.

DIP STICK
CLEANER

Time to check the oil? Why wipe the murky mess on your sleeve or your lips? Your multiple use bandanna can do the trick.

41.

HOT SEAT

PREVENTER

Why spend money on one of those ungainly window shades for your windshield? A bandanna snugly tucked into each bucket seat is much handier - not to mention, a smart look.

✪ ✪ ✪

42. & 43.

Got a leaky
radiator? 👉

This is better than a mechanic. Just stop the leak with a bandanna and get to your nearest repair shop.

Ever have a
wiper blade fail you?

Just slide your bandanna under the blade, and drive worry free. But get it fixed before the next rain drop falls.

44.

BETTER THAN
A HANDY
WIPE

A bandanna is perfect for the incidental messes any driver has to deal with, whether it be dealing with wiping off bird poop, mopping up fast-food spills, getting the steam off a windshield after a few hours of smooching your best girl. It's an all-purpose cleaning cloth. And will never tell your secrets.

* *

45.

Tie the
CAR DOOR
SHUT

It's not unheard of that friendly rough-housing, a night of heavy drinking or an irate girlfriend can result in a broken car door. The bandanna is the perfect length and size to fix that problem, and at least get you home without having to hold the door shut with your left hand.

46.

CAR MAT
COVERS

Just shampooed your car carpets? Don't
let your friends spill latte all over them.
Place your bandannas on the mats,
snugly fit around the edges, until the
shampoo dries. Then tell your friends to
walk home.

✪   ✪   ✪

★ ★ ★ ★ ★ ★ ★ ★ ★ ★ ★ ★ ★ ★ ★ ★ ★ ★ ★ ★

47.

CARRYALL

FOR IMPORTANT

vehicular documents

There isn't much worse than rifling through your glove compartment while a policeman holds the flashlight through your driver side window. Easiest way to find what you need it to keep it all wrapped in a bandanna. Might even save you from spending time behind bars.

✪ ✪ ✪

48.

Steering
WHEEL
COVER

Forget lambs wool. Try bandannas to cover your steering wheel. This will take two, but wrap them around the wheel, and use a shoelace, plastic twist ties or thin leather straps to keep them in place. This should take you about six hours to do.

49.

CAR

window shade

If you have any more bandannas left from the last diaper change, tape one to the back passenger side window, covering its entire surface, so that Junior can finally get some rest. Resist the temptation to listen to lullabies, since you might pass out, too.

★ ★

50.
TRAILER
HITCH

Keeping in line with good driver-ship, tying a bandanna to the back of your hitch notifies other motorists of the possibly deadly metal object sticking out of the back your vehicle which threatens to rip open the undercarriage of theirs if they are tailgating.

✪ ✪ ✪

51.

KEY RING

Tie your keys to your wrist with your bandanna, especially if you're prone to misplacing them or dropping them accidentally down an open sewer.

★ ★ ★

AROUND THE HOUSE

OH THE AMAZING DECORATING YOU CAN DO WITH BANDANNAS

Not to mention the multitude of practical uses.

★ ★ ★ ★ ★ ★ ★ ★ ★ ★ ★ ★ ★ ★ ★ ★ ★ ★ ★ ★

52.

A FESTIVE THROW PILLOW

✳ Couch looking a bit barren? ✳
Try a bandanna pillow.

How to do it:

Lay out two bandanas, wrong sides together. Cut 3" slits
3"all around the bandana every 3/4" (Figure 1). Cut out the
corners (Figure 2). Flip so right sides are now facing out.
Lay a small pillow form between the two bandanas lining up
the cut slits (Figure 3). Tie the fringes and voila (Figure 4).

★ ★

1.

2.

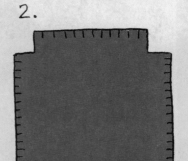

3.

4.

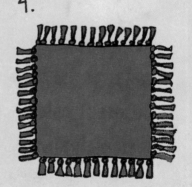

PRESTO!

53.

DRESS UP

YOUR TABLE

with paisley

Bandannas make great napkins and place mats, as is. Rip another bandanna of a different color into three-inch by one-inch strips, and tie around the middle of the napkin. Adds that rustic, rough-and-ready feel to any party table.

★ ★ ★

★ ★ ★ ★ ★ ★ ★ ★ ★ ★ ★ ★ ★ ★ ★ ★ ★ ★ ★ ★

54.

FRAME ME

There isn't a picture frame around that couldn't stand to have a bandanna make over. All it takes is glue and patience. Place the picture frame on the reverse side of the bandanna. Cut a hole in the middle with enough fabric to pull through to the other side. Cut slits on the diagonal. Glue them to the opposite side of the frame. Pull the remaining fabric around the edges, trim fabric and glue in place.

✪ ✪ ✪

55.

Lid covers

Tired of all those boring jars of pickled beets with those tinny looking covers? Ugh. Take a bandanna, cut it into eight squares, secure them on each cover with a rubber band, and place them back in your cupboard. Or better yet, display them on your window sill for guests to oooh and ahhhh over. For even more fun, cover any ugly jar in your fridge or cupboard by reversing the process. Show your canning pride.

56.
LIGHT BULB CHANGERS

The days of singeing your fingertips are over. A bandanna bunched up in your hand has amazing grippage. It can also be used to pry open stubborn jar lids and as a dusting rag in a pinch.

57.

Wine bottle
APRON

What's better than wrapping a linen napkin around your 1787 Chateau Lafite when you serve it? (Probably not serving it all.) But if you have to, why not indulge your wild side and wrap a bandanna around it instead. After all, expensive wine speaks for itself. But you can add the outerwear.

★ ★

58.
TUPPERWARE ALTERNATIVE

No, not for storing anything. Think more along the lines of using as a playful way to give away a batch of homemade cookies, wrap around a hot loaf of crusty bread or line an old, tired, plastic storage container. Perk up your miserable life.

★ ★ ★

59.

Gardener's KNEE PADS

Knees on your pants crusted with mud? Well, put away the stain remover. Just tie a bandanna around each knee, and go jump into the soil.

★ ★

60.
PLANT
❀ TIES ❀

Why use boring string or cheesy twist ties? Give your garden a splash of color and the mark of your personality. Rip a bandanna in strips and use that to hold back your tomato plants.

★ ★ ★

61.

PLANT
identifiers

It's so confusing in the garden if you don't remember what you planted where. Try a simple coded system for your garden: a green bandanna for peppers, red for tomatoes, yellow for zucchini (make sure you only plant one of those), orange for carrots and purple for kumquats.

62.

ITCH THIS

Sensitive to poison ivy?

Well, you don't have to touch it ever again, or ruin a pair of expensive garden gloves by pulling out the unwanted weeds. Wrap a bandanna around your hand, and knot at the wrist. After you manhandle the itchy weed and show it who's boss, throw the bandanna away to prevent spreading.

✪ ✪ ✪

★ ★ ★ ★ ★ ★ ★ ★ ★ ★ ★ ★ ★ ★ ★ ★ ★ ★ ★

63.

LUGGAGE
✸ TAG ✸

Who doesn't have problems identifying their black wheeled luggage at the airport? Not you. Tie a bandanna securely around the handle and just wait at the carousel for yours to appear. You might even start a trend.

✪ ✪ ✪

64.

EYEGLASS CLEANER

Nothing is quite as soft as a well-worn bandanna. So soft in fact that it can be used to get the schmootz off your sensitive eyeglasses without concern of scratching or marring the lenses.

★ ★ ★

65.

EGG
separator

Forget the cheese cloth. Try wetting a fresh bandanna and letting the fabric act as a natural method to separate out the egg whites for that perfect meringue. Or use it to filter out unfiltered water. Leave the rust in the bandanna and use it for your next hobo trip.

66.

ESCAPE
route 👉

Worried about how to exit your house without an emergency ladder? Worry no more. You can knot a bunch of bandannas together to escape a burning house, escape from jail or just sneak out for the night. Note: Best to use this method when you live on the first floor.

★ ★ ★

★ ★

67.

Guest gag

Who hasn't wanted to end the pain of a know-it-all bore at a house party? **A bandanna, scrunched up, is the perfect size to silence the most annoying of guests. Just stuff it in the offender's mouth, and laugh uproariously. Guests and friends alike will appreciate the jocularity and revel in the fun of the moment. And you won't have to worry about Mr. Boring ever darkening your doorstep again.**

★ ★

68.

BEER
CADDY

Not enough room in the fridge for your booze? Pack your bandanna with small ice slivers and a six of beer, knot the end, leaving an opening big enough to pull out a can or two, and hang it on the doorknob to the garage door.

★ ★ ★

69.

CALICO
CURTAINS

Oh, you'll need a lot of bandannas for this, and a sewing machine. But it's worth it when you see the happy looks on your family's faces when they see the lovely drapes and window dressings you have whipped up out of bandannas. It's worth the 72 hours of sewing. Too much? Just try stitching your bandannas into festive tie-backs for your other drapes.

70.

SHOE
stuffer

Don't worry about finding a shoe tree
for all your fine leather shoes. Just stuff
your bandannas inside the toes, secure
in the knowledge that they will fit next
time you wear them.

✪ ✪ ✪

★ ★ ★ ★ ★ ★ ★ ★ ★ ★ ★ ★ ★ ★ ★ ★ ★ ★ ★ ★

71.

Polly want some privacy?

Your bird needs some space and downtime.
And so do you. Use your favorite bandanna
as a bird cage cover and keep the feathered
beast quiet for the night.

★ ★ ★

★ ★

72.

POTPOURRI HOLDER

Take your bandanna and stuff it with some sweet smelling lavender, Queen Anne's lace, coffee grounds and old wrestler's socks. Use it in drawers or closets to add fragrance to your life.

★ ★ ★

73.

Mr. Muffin NEEDS A TOY

And he loves cat nip. So have a ball driving him crazy with a bandanna ball stuffed with his favorite addictive herb.

74.

OOOPS,
out of filters

Bandannas also have the handy ability to help out Mr. Coffee in a pinch. Just line the plastic drip dispenser with a bandanna, fill it with coffee and hit "on."

Tea time

If tea is your poison of choice, then use your bandanna as a tea ball replacement. Note: One bandanna can make enough tea to service the country of Lithuania.

★ ★

75.

SHELF
LINER

Boring best describes the shelf liners on the market today. Spiff up your kitchen design by adding calico to your shelves. This even works in the refrigerator and acts as a nifty spill collector.

✪ ✪ ✪

★ ★ ★ ★ ★ ★ ★ ★ ★ ★ ★ ★ ★ ★ ★ ★ ★ ★ ★ ★

76.

POT
holder

In a pinch, don't use your sleeve or the wet dish towel (ouch) to pull a steaming hot casserole out of the oven. Grab your bandannas, would you?

77.

LAMP SHADE

Any new mommy knows the trick of dimming the lampshade with a scarf. Well, what about draping a bandanna? Let the kid know his roots early on.

★ ★ ★

EEW KOOTIES

Appeal to your inner germ-a-phobe.

Use the bandanna to pick up the telephone, cover the toilet seat in a public place, or reach for a door handle. Never come in contact with another germ again. Even wear one when you shake hands.

79. & 80.

Shoe polisher

With a little spit, your bandanna rivals the best shoe polish in town.

Camera lens CLEANER

Softer than most fabrics, the bandanna doesn't run the risk of marking your expensive lens. Just make sure you didn't blow your nose in it first.

★ ★ ★ ★ ★ ★ ★ ★ ★ ★ ★ ★ ★ ★ ★ ★ ★ ★ ★ ★

81.

THE ULTIMATE GIFT

Fits the bill for someone who has everything, someone who has nothing, or someone who just needs a bandanna.

★ ★ ★

★ ★

HEY LOOK AT ME!

SOME OF US JUST NEED TO BE NOTICED

And bandannas, because of their versatility, shout autonomy and speak to the greater need in all of us to be different.

82.

Stand out in a crowd

Meeting friends at the theatre, flagging down a taxi or just desperate for attention, try tying a brightly colored bandanna on a stick and waving it. Believe it or not, crowds will indeed gather.

✪ ✪ ✪

83.

MOVIE THEATER
SEAT
SAVER

In your desperate rush to find the best seat in the house, you bypass the popcorn stand. Leave your bandanna royally displayed, and you can head back to gather up your bucket of heart clogging, palm-oil infused popcorn, loaded with faux butter and salt.

★ ★ ★ ★ ★ ★ ★ ★ ★ ★ ★ ★ ★ ★ ★ ★ ★ ★ ★

84.

Broken ARM?

Or just pretending to have one, the bandanna is the ultimate sling or tourniquet. And it does the trick to express your inner desire to dare to be different.

✪ ✪ ✪

85.

PACK
your lunch

Why invest in a lunch pack? Use a bandanna to handily wrap your baguette and goat cheese for work. When you're all done, you can wipe the crumbs off your face with it.

★ ★ ★

* *

86.

NECK
cover up

Whether it be an unsightly hickey or a scar from your recent trip to the plastic surgeon, a bandanna can fit neatly around one's neck, calling attention to it in an oh-so-subtle way.

★ ★ ★

87.

Personal DISTRESS SIGNAL

If you're the shy type–and even if you're not–you can use the handy bandanna to alert your mate that you're ready for sex. You could even get fancy, and pick colors for codes of whatever it is you are interested in at the time.

88.

Making a BALD MAN ✳ COOL ✳

The bandanna should be singlehandedly credited for adding a bit of couture to those whose scalps are lacking. What bald man hasn't donned a bandanna, knotted smartly in the back, to protect his thinning or exposed pate from the sun. If this doesn't say 'look at me,' what does?

89.

BANNER
waving

Carrying a spare bandanna, especially if you are an athlete, comes in handy when you want to rub it in the face of your opponent. If you win, you can run around waving your bandanna like an obnoxious person. If you lose, you can use it for weeping profusely.

★ ★ ★ ★ ★ ★ ★ ★ ★ ★ ★ ★ ★ ★ ★ ★ ★ ★ ★ ★

90.

MALE ENHANCER

Tired of being pointed at and made fun of? Stuff a bandanna - no, two - down your pants. Show 'em who's the man.

✪ ✪ ✪

★ ★

91.

MOLOTOV cocktail

Perfect for the anarchist in you. Soak your bandanna in a little kerosene, stuff it in a glass bottle, and you're all set. Note: Please don't try this at home. We are, after all, professionals.

✪ ✪ ✪

★ ★

92.

Carrying
POUCH

If you really like to be noticed, make a
small sling for around your neck to act as a
neck fanny pack. You can keep your wallet,
personal items and keys close to your mouth.
Or you could fill it with granola for a snack,
something akin to a feedbag.

✪ ✪ ✪

★ ★

93.

PUDDLE JUMPER

Let the gentleman in you shine. Lay your freshly pressed bandanna over the nearest puddle and let your damsel saunter across, keeping her shoes dry and feet fresh.

✪ ✪ ✪

★ ★ ★ ★ ★ ★ ★ ★ ★ ★ ★ ★ ★ ★ ★ ★ ★ ★ ★ ★

94.
WIND SOCKET

Sailor or not, everyone needs to know what direction the wind is blowing. You can make a small wind socket by gathering the four ends of your bandanna, and placing it (and caution) in the wind. Note: If it blows violently out of your hand, run for cover, a hurricane is on the way.

★ ★ ★ ★ ★ ★ ★ ★ ★ ★ ★ ★ ★ ★ ★ ★ ★ ★ ★

95.

TORTURE USES

A bandanna, with the very tip dipped in ice water, makes a mean rat tail, with just the right amount of snap. Twisted into a rope, it can act as a pair of hand-cuffs, or a garrotte. Note: Please do not try this at home. We are professionals.

96.

Make a bandanna map

Draw where you are going on your bandanna, which you can then keep as a keepsake. You can also draw lots of attention when staring blankly at it in St. Peter's square. Look at it this way - you are never lost with a map around your neck.

✪ ✪ ✪

97.

PLAY

TUG OF WAR

What better way to pick someone up?

Rather than chatting, make merry and show off your physical prowess with a rousing game of tug of war. Winner takes all.

✪ ✪ ✪

★ ★

98.

Weapon for BIBLICAL fights

On the off chance you might be coming up on
Goliath any day soon, keep a bandanna at the
ready, with a supply of rocks. Just in case.

★ ★

99.

Survival

OF THE MOST

COLORFUL

Bandannas have been the constant companion of outdoorsmen for years. Use them to mark a trail, wipe the sweat from the brow, wet in a stream for instant relief, wrap around the arm for snake bite venom removal, spray one with repellent and let it hang from your belt, a bear bag when hiking, or use it as replacement toilet paper.

* *

100.

LOIN CLOTH

Run around buck naked, with a bit of leather or string keeping your bandanna loosely in place. There is no end to the fun you can have. Note: Please feel free to try to this at home.

CHAPTER 4

(AND 3 MORE USES!)

NOW THAT YOU'VE HAD A TASTE OF JUST A FEW OF THE THINGS YOUR NEW BANDANNA CAN DO FOR YOU,

the ideas should be filling your head and spilling out onto the floor by now. Let them run around for a few minutes before you gather them up. Make sure you keep them separated by gender because ideas, like rabbits, can proliferate pretty quickly. And we can't have that now, can we? Hoisting your bandanna high over your head, you can now move boldly forward in trying out some of these ideas. Through it all, make sure you take good care of your new charge. The care and keeping of your bandanna is very simple. Just toss it in the wash. Like blue jeans and your boyfriend, some things are meant to be worn out. A bandanna is one of them. Wash it a million times, and notice how soft it gets. But over time, it will start to fall apart. When that happens, there are still some more things you can do with it.

CREATE A FAMILY HEIRLOOM

When it gets a little too threadbare, start making a quilt. By the time you're 90, you can hand it down to the next generation and the generation after that, recalling the grand old times you had with your bandanna. Take a quilting class before embarking on this venture.

MAKE LOCKET MEMENTOES

Cut it into little pieces, and save the little bits in separate lockets for your grandchildren. Tell them some tall tale about the fabric in the locket. Create a history for yourself that never was, secure in the knowledge that it will be passed down through the generations after you are gone, and everyone will think you were just the coolest.

HOST A BANDANNA BURIAL

Too little paisley left? Honor a bandanna that has had a life well lived. Invite friends and family over, showing off your best bandanna finery. Gather round the funeral pyre, playing Taps on your kazoos, and solemnly burn your old friend. Free its spirit into the universe. Cremation not your thing? Bury it in the backyard with Fido.

★ ★ ★

YOUR BANDANNA CAN BE THE BEST THING THAT EVER HAPPENED TO YOU. BUT FIRST, YOU HAVE TO TIE ONE ON. GO AHEAD! YOU CAN DO IT.

★ ★

ABOUT
CIDER MILL PRESS
Book Publishers

Good ideas ripen with time. From seed to harvest, Cider Mill Press strives to bring fine reading, information, and entertainment together between the covers of its creatively crafted books. Our Cider Mill bears fruit twice a year, publishing a new crop of titles each spring and fall.

Where good books
are ready for press

VISIT US ON THE WEB AT
www.cidermillpress.com

OR WRITE TO US AT
12 Port Farm Road
Kennebunkport, Maine 04046